WANDSWORTH AND BATTERSEA TRAMWAYS

Robert J Harley

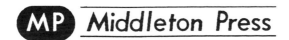

MP Middleton Press

> Cover Picture: A service 34 tram and a taxicab wait for the green light at the foot of Beaufort Street, Chelsea in the early post-war years.   (R.Elliott)
>
> Cover Colours: These reflect the livery applied to London Transport tramcars.

First published October 1995

ISBN 1 873793 63 4

© Middleton Press 1995

Design - Deborah Goodridge

Published by Middleton Press
              Easebourne Lane
              Midhurst
              West Sussex
              GU29 9AZ
              Tel: 01730 813169

Printed & bound by Biddles Ltd,
              Guildford and Kings Lynn

CONTENTS

INTRODUCTION AND ACKNOWLEDGEMENTS

In the Tramway Classics series I have endeavoured to bring to life a past era of quality public transport. However, I would also like readers to remember that many cities in the world still rely on modern tramcars for safe travel which enhances the environment at street level. If we really want to get people moving in urban Britain we need to employ the technology of up to date light rail systems such as have recently appeared in Manchester and Sheffield. I hope the following views from a bygone age will stimulate some thinking on our present day traffic problems.

Our journey in pictures has been make possible by the following photographers and collectors of old postcards, my thanks go to: Alan Cross, Gerald Druce, Richard Elliott, John Gillham, H.B.Priestley, D.Trevor Rowe, Don Thompson and Richard Wiseman. The work of John Meredith has featured throughout the series, and I wish to express my thanks and the gratitude of many satisfied readers for all his efforts in producing and supplying photos for publication. My task has also been made easier by the unstinting support of John Price who has contributed much information to the series. He has also been able to lend many rare postcard views. Pictures from the collections of the late V.E.Burrows, W.A.Camwell, N.N.Forbes, F.Merton Atkins, R.B.Parr, K.H.Rudolph and G.N.Southerden appear in this book and many of these photos have been loaned by Dave Jones. Terry Russell has again supplied one of his superb drawings for the rolling stock section. Much detailed information has been gleaned from two volumes on the London County Council Tramways by E.R.Oakley and from a series of articles by C.S.Dunbar which appeared in Tramway Review in 1969/70.

GEOGRAPHICAL SETTING

The River Wandle flows into the Thames at Wandsworth and along the two rivers a chain of villages has evolved. These settlements along country roads in North Surrey have developed over the years and now form an extension of the metropolis. Only a few areas such as Wandsworth Common and Battersea Park have escaped urbanisation. The landscape in this part of South London is dominated by the intricate pattern of railway lines, many of them elevated above street level. Putney faces the Fulham district across the Thames and the main road runs northwards parallel to the river until it reaches Hammersmith.

HISTORICAL BACKGROUND

Wandsworth was the northern terminus of the Surrey Iron Railway which opened in July 1803. This horse worked line, built to convey freight, was eventually extended to Croydon and the North Downs at Merstham. Although passengers were not carried, the track was laid across and by the side of several local roads. More conventional steam railways reached the area in 1838 with the opening of the line from Nine Elms to Southampton.

Horse tramways running in the street appeared on the scene in 1881 with the inauguration of the first sections of the South London Tramways Co along the "bottom road"- Battersea Park Road. Falcon Road and the stretch between Chelsea Bridge and Wandsworth Road via Queens Road were also traversed by horse cars. Progress in construction then picked up and the "top road" from East Hill Wandsworth, serving Lavender Hill and Wandsworth Road, opened in June 1882. Connections to the rest of the South London network via Nine Elms Lane and Wandsworth Road followed in 1883. Further lines were also laid in Wandsworth to terminate in North Street. Across the river in Hammersmith, horse trams of the West Metropolitan Co. entered the town in July 1883 thus providing a direct connection to Kew Bridge.

The London County Council purchased the South London operations in November 1902, with the result that tramcars were repainted and renumbered by the new owners. The services acquired by the LCC were as follows:

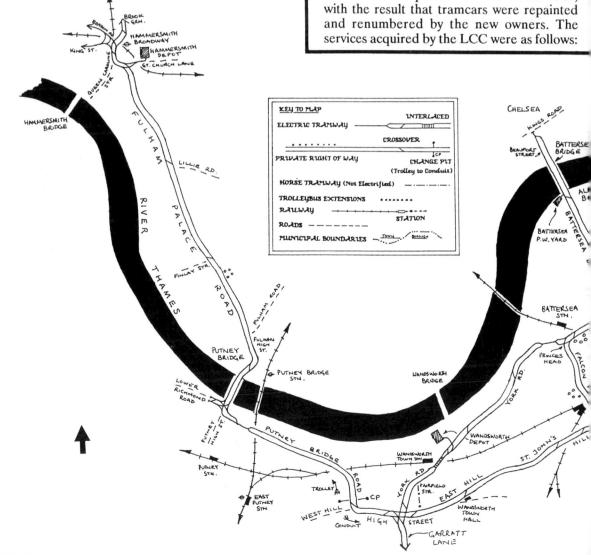

East Hill to Hop Exchange (Brown)
East Hill to Westminster Stangate (Yellow)
North Street to Hop Exchange (Green)
North Street to Westminster (Blue)
Lavender Hill to Chelsea Bridge (Red)
Clapham Junction, Falcon Road to Chelsea Bridge (Chocolate)

As was common practice in company days, the cars bore different colours for the various routes and these are indicated in brackets.

At the turn of the century the trend throughout the world was towards tramways powered by electricity, and the progressive London United Tramways, guided by the forceful James Clifton Robinson, was not slow off the mark. On 4th April 1901 the brand new LUT trams began serving Hammersmith. In the County of London, plans were being quickly formulated for the conversion; the preferred method in the LCC area was the underground conduit system which was very expensive, but had the aesthetic advantage of not requiring overhead wires (A fuller technical description can be found in companion volume *Embankment and Waterloo Tramways*). Although the council had the best intentions in providing Londoners with cheap and efficient transport, plans for extensions across the Thames into the West End were always challenged by the London General Omnibus Company who had the support of many rich and powerful factions. This opposition explains the gap in tramway communications at the heart of the metropolis.

In 1906 electric trams reached Wandsworth from Tooting; the reconstructed depot at Jews Row, Wandsworth was opened on 12th October the same year. The horse tramway in North Street was replaced by new electric tracks incorporated into a western extension of York Road. Further lines were inaugurated in Falcon Road, Battersea Park Road, Nine Elms Lane and Wandsworth Road to Vauxhall Cross. In January 1909 single deck cars commenced operation along Queens Road to the southern end of Chelsea Bridge. These vehicles were used because of the restricted headroom under several railway bridges which precluded the usual double deck operation. Meanwhile, construction was proceeding apace on the "top road" and the through electric service from East Hill began on 15th December 1909. A useful new link to Clapham via Cedars Road was added on 26th February 1910.

The LCC did have one major success in establishing an important cross-London route when parliamentary powers were obtained for a service from Harlesden in the north west, to Hammersmith and Putney, crossing the Thames at Putney Bridge. The Hammersmith to Harlesden section opened for traffic in May 1908 and the complete route was equipped with overhead wires. In the previous month Hammersmith Depot received its first electric trams for the new services. South of Hammersmith, the terminus in Lower Richmond Road, Putney, was reached in January 1909. Tracks in Putney Bridge Road were made operational in January 1912, and they were extended to within a few yards of Wandsworth High Street where a change pit to effect the transfer of cars from the overhead to the conduit was installed.

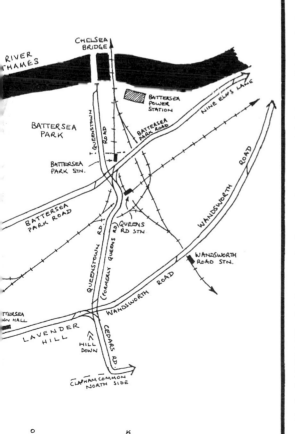

Services for January 1915 as shown on the accompanying map extract:

12 Tooting Junction to Hop Exchange
14 Tooting Junction to Victoria Embankment
26 East Hill to Hop Exchange
28 East Hill to Victoria
30 East Hill to Waterloo Station
32 Lavender Hill to Chelsea Bridge
34 Clapham Junction to Kings Road, Chelsea
82 Harrow Road, Harlesden to High Street,
                           Wandsworth
86 Clapham Junction to Waterloo Bridge

Although service 82 ran for most of its length north of the Thames, it was included in the South London series as an even numbered service.

The Putney Bridge Road link up with the York Road and Garratt Lane lines occurred in July 1915. Finally in August 1921, the rails were extended past the East Hill terminus to form a junction with the York Road/Garratt Lane routes. A connection between the LCC and LUT lines was inserted at Hammersmith in May 1922.

The May 1925 LCC tram map shows a substantial rearrangement of services due to new lines and through running agreements. Local services were as follows:
12 Tooting Junction to Hop Exchange
14 Earlsfield Station to Hop Exchange
26 Kew Bridge to Hop Exchange
28 Harrow Road, Harlesden to Victoria Station
30 Sudbury to Tooting Junction
32 Lavender Hill to Chelsea Bridge
34 Kings Road, Chelsea to Southwark Bridge
82 Harrow Road, Harlesden to Tooting Junction

This pattern of services remained largely unaltered until the formation of London Transport in 1933. The only major change of note before this, was the lowering of the roadway under the railway bridges in Queen's Road on 3rd May 1926. This permitted the use of double deck cars on service 32 which was extended to the Plough, Clapham in November 1927. Service 14 was extended in April 1931

Extract from LCC tram map January 1915

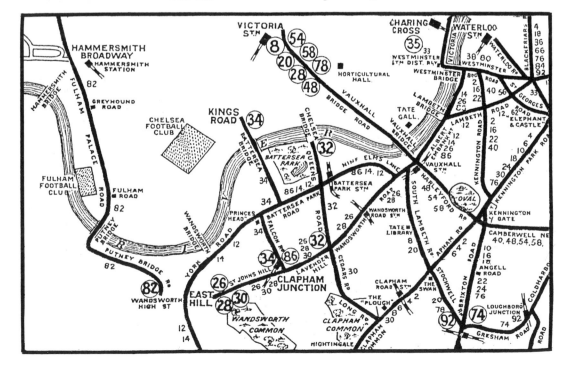

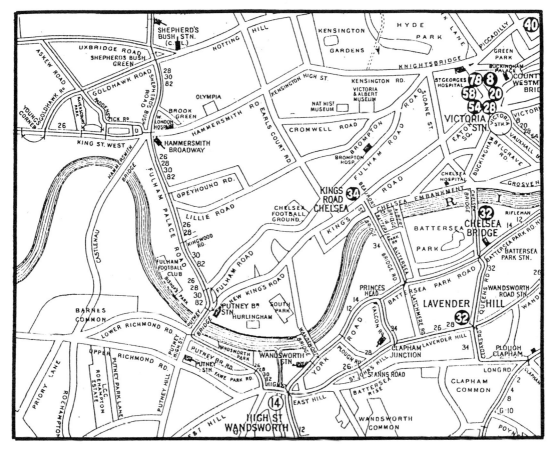

Extract from LCC tram map May 1925

over former LUT tracks in Haydons Road to Wimbledon Hill Road (More information on this service is contained in the Middleton Press album *Kingston and Wimbledon Tramways*).

The London Transport regime proved fatal to the capital's tramways. In a very short time it became apparent that the whole network was under threat. First to go was the service 14 extension along Haydons Road which succumbed to the motor bus in 1934. The following year saw numbers of workmen on the streets of West London engaged in erecting new traction standards and wiring for trolleybuses. Partial conversion of the Wandsworth tram services occurred in September 1937; tracks were abandoned in East Hill, Garratt Lane and from the High Street to Harlesden via Putney and Hammersmith. Trams still operated from Wandsworth Depot, along York Road and from Clapham Junction to Central London, but many of the benefits of through services were lost when passengers had to change vehicles. The remaining tramway services were scheduled for later replacement by trolleybuses, however the Second World War intervened. In that time of national emergency, the trams really came into their own; they performed sterling service throughout the blitz and the years of austerity after the war. But they were living on borrowed time and inevitably the conversion programme resumed as soon as the requisite number of motor buses, now the favoured replacement, could be delivered. In 1950 the axe fell on the Wandsworth and Battersea areas, with the last trams operating on 30th September. Trolleybus route 612 also perished on the same day; the era of electric street traction finally ended when all the other local trolleybuses were replaced by diesel buses in 1960.

1. We begin our journey in Nine Elms Lane where car 1946 has just negotiated the cross-over by Everett Street. The tracks further east are described in companion Middleton Press volume *Victoria and Lambeth Tramways*. (J.H.Meredith)

2. A sunny June day in 1949 sees car 1928 pausing at a tram stop which is conveniently attached to the traffic light post. This scene is framed by the arch of the bridge which carries railway tracks into Battersea Park Station. In the roadway can be noticed the remains of the former junction with service 32 and the curves that led from Battersea Park Road into Queen's Road, later renamed Queenstown Road. (J.H.Meredith)

3. North of the junction in the previous photo, we encounter a standard LCC eight wheel car at Chelsea Bridge terminus. Service 32 was known to the crews as the "chicken run"; it was normally worked by four trams with an extra car in peak hours. Unfortunately this tramway disappeared on 8th September 1937 when it was replaced by a strengthened bus route 137. (C.F.Klapper)

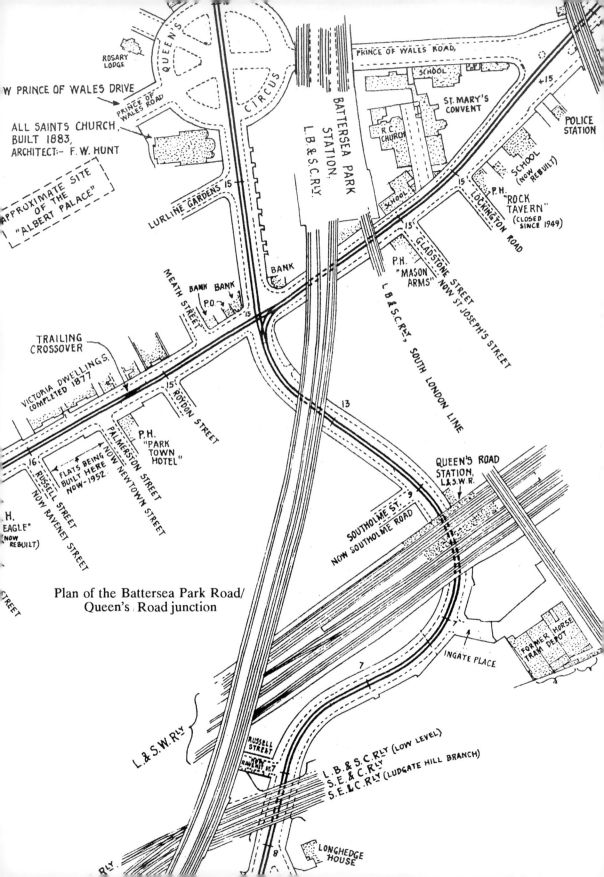

Plan of the Battersea Park Road/
Queen's Road junction

4. The photographer has now positioned himself at the very end of the track. Note the section feeder box on the pavement to the right of the tram. Both horse tramway (opened in 1881) and electric replacement (opened in 1909) failed to reach the real traffic objectives on the other bank of the Thames. This was mainly due to powerful opposition by the "carriage folk" on the Chelsea side. (C.F.Klapper)

5.   At least potential passengers had the benefit of a shelter in the event of inclement weather. Here LT car 1043 rests before the return trip to the Plough, Clapham. (A.B.Cross)

6.   Not long before abandonment, car 1050 is pictured with Chelsea Bridge in the background. The original suspension bridge was opened on 30th March 1858 and was upgraded to cope with the increased motor traffic in 1935-37. One of the entrances to Battersea Park can be seen to the left of the picture. This well known recreational spot for Londoners contains a large lake which was laid out in 1860. Many acres of parkland are dissected by drives and these were popular haunts for fashionable cyclists of the 1890s; the park roads were also favourites for many early motorists as they practised their skills before emerging on to the public highway. (R.Elliott)

7.   We return in the direction of Battersea Park Road in company with LCC car 570. The overhead wires of the electrified railway of the former LBSC company can be seen to the right of the tram. More details of this operation are to be found in Middleton Press album *South London Line*.   (F.Merton Atkins)

8.   Near the junction of Queen's Road with South Street, a single deck car passes under one of the three railway bridges which crossed this part of the route between Battersea Park Road and Lavender Hill. Double deck operation commenced on 6th November 1927 after the highway had been lowered under the two other bridges further along the road. (R.J.Harley Coll.)

9. This scene outside St.Philips Church appeared on a local postcard produced before the First World War. The tram in the foreground, car 601, was the last vehicle of class G. These cars are fully described in *Embankment and Waterloo Tramways*. They were once also associated with services using the Kingsway Subway. (D.Jones Coll.)

10. Nearing the end of its journey along Queen's Road, a tram slows for the curves leading towards the Cedars Road/Lavender Hill crossroads. This junction is further illustrated in pictures 54-57. (J.H.Price Coll.)

BATTERSEA PARK ROAD
TO KINGS ROAD, CHELSEA

11. Car 1810 passes a milk float in Battersea Park Road. This tram was normally housed in Clapham Depot, but here it seems to have been "lent" to help out on service 12. The date is 23rd September 1950. (J.H.Meredith)

WITHDRAWAL OF TRAM ROUTE 32.

On Wednesday, September 8th, Route 32 tram (Clapham Common and Chelsea Bridge) will be withdrawn, and Bus Route No. 137 will operate between these points.

The following transfer fares will be withdrawn :—

5d. Ordinary Return—

John Carpenter Street and Chelsea Bridge ...
Borough Road Railway Bridge and Chelsea Bridge

4d. Workman and 6d. Ordinary Return— ⎬ Change at Queens Road, Battersea Park Road.

Hop Exchange and Chelsea Bridge ... ...
Goswell Road and Chelsea Bridge ... ...

2d. Cheap Mid-day—

Hop Exchange and Chelsea Bridge ... ...   Change at Queens Road, Battersea Park Road, or Lavender Hill.

Victoria and Chelsea Bridge ... ...   Change at Queens Road, Lavender Hill.
Southampton Row and Chelsea Bridge ... ...   Change at Queens Road, Battersea Park Road.
Embankment ... ...
City via Southwark ... ... ⎬ and Chelsea ⎬ Change at Clapham Common Station.
Blackfriars via Camberwell ...   Bridge
Victoria ... ...

ROUTE No. 32.

Victoria Embankment (John Carpenter Street) and King's Road, Chelsea, to Clapham Junction (Electric Traction).

1. City of London School.
2. Sion College.
3. Metropolitan Asylums Board Offices.
4. The Temple.
5. L.C.C. Education Offices.
6. Somerset House.
7. Savoy Theatre.
8. Charing Cross Station.
9. Trafalgar Square.
10. New Scotland Yard.
11. Houses of Parliament.
12. Westminster Abbey.
13. St. Thomas' Hospital.
14. Archbishop's Park.
15. Lambeth Palace.
16. Kennington Oval.
17. Devas Institute.
18. Battersea Polytechnic.
19. Battersea Parish Church.
20. Crosby Hall.
21. Chelsea Old Church.
22. Carlyle Museum.
23. Chelsea Embankment Gardens.

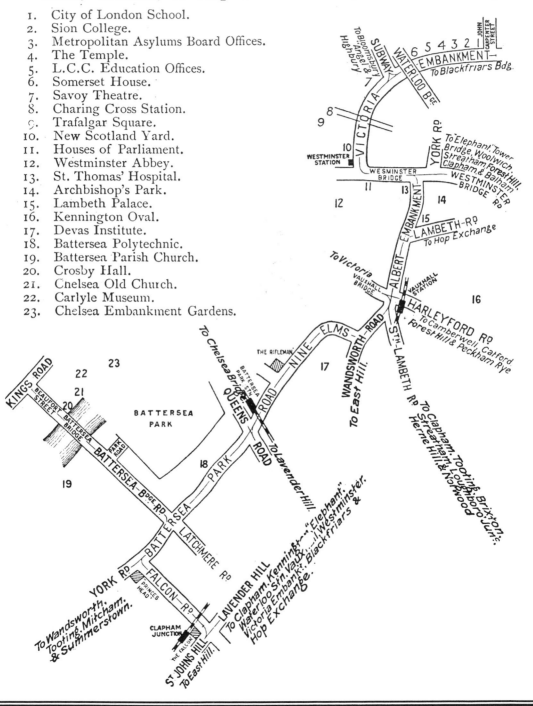

12. Outside Segalls the Drapers in Battersea Park Road the traffic consists of car 364 which is being pursued by a splendid looking vintage lorry. The piles in the roadway, so beloved of rose growers, indicate one of the environmental drawbacks of horse drawn traffic. (J.H.Price Coll.)

13. Two vehicles belonging to the Central Road Services division of London Transport are pictured in Battersea Park Road at its junction with Battersea Bridge Road. Car 1954 is on a short working to Westminster which will not entail a trip through the Kingsway Subway to the usual terminus of service 31 at Islington Green. The tracks in this picture were closed to trams from 30th September 1950 and lifting commenced the next month. Proposals for reinstating a tram service to carry passengers to the Festival of Britain Pleasure Gardens at Battersea Park came to nothing. In the event, special bus routes were used from May to November 1951. (J.H.Meredith)

14. In this view the former east to north curves from Battersea Park Road to Battersea Bridge Road can be seen. This is the last day of trams at this spot and tomorrow the motorists will have the road to themselves. (J.C.Gillham)

15. A warning about the closure of Battersea Bridge is fixed to the traffic light on the island as car 189 waits to turn right out of the lane reserved for northbound traffic. Conflicting movements between trams and other road vehicles caused by badly positioned traffic refuges were nearly always blamed on the trams. (J.H.Meredith)

16. Battersea Bridge Road and car 1103 on service 34 heads for Camberwell Green. This particular tram had an interesting history. It was badly damaged in an accident on Westhorne Avenue, Eltham in March 1934, and it was rebuilt with a modernised top deck and flush sides in May of the same year. The most notable feature from a passenger's point of view was the provision of comfortable, upholstered, swivelling seats in both the upper and lower saloons. (D.Trevor Rowe)

LT timetable for service 34, December 1943

ROUTE 34	Chelsea - Clapham - Camberwell - Blackfriars	P.M. times are in heavy figures

Via Beaufort Street, Battersea Bridge, Battersea Park Road, Falcon Road, Lavender Hill, Cedars Road, Long Road, Clapham High Street, Clapham Road, Stockwell Road, Gresham Road, Coldharbour Lane, Denmark Hill, Camberwell Road, Walworth Road, London Road, Blackfriars Road, Blackfriars Bridge.

RAILWAY STATIONS SERVED : Clapham Junction, Clapham Common, Clapham SR, Clapham North, Stockwell, East Brixton, Loughborough Junction, Elephant and Castle, Blackfriars.

Service interval : Chelsea–Camberwell WEEKDAYS 4–6 mins. (evening 12 mins.), SUNDAY, morn. 12 mins., aft. 6 mins., eve. 12 mins. Camberwell–Blackfriars WEEKDAYS 10 mins. (peak hours 4 mins., Saturday afternoon 8 mins., evenings 12 mins.), SUNDAY 12 mins.

	WEEKDAYS First		SO	SX			SUNDAY First				DAILY Last SO		
CHELSEA *Kings Road*	....	....	....	5 8	5 22	5 29	....	....	8 50	....	..	9 31	9 43	11 5
Clapham Junction	..	X4 46	..	5 8	5 20	5 34	5 41	....	8 19	8 59	..	9 43	9 55	11 17
Clapham Common Stn., *Underground*	4 7	4 51	4 58	5 18	5 30	5 44	5 51	†8 5	8 28	9 8	..	9 53	10 5	11 27
Brixton Road *Stockwell Road*	4 16	5 2	5 9	5 29	5 41	5 55	6 2	..	8 15	8 37	9 17	..	10 4	10 16	..
Camberwell Green	4 25	5 12	5 19	5 39	5 51	6 5	6 12	..	8 24	8 46	9 26	..	10 14	10 26	..
BLACKFRIARS *John Carpenter St.*	..	..	5 39	5 59	6 11	6 25	6 32	..	8 41	9 3	9 43	..	10 34	..	..
BLACKFRIARS *John Carpenter St.*	....	..	5 40	6 0	....	....	..	....	8 43	....	....	....	10 6	10 36	....
Camberwell Green	..	4 28	6 0	6 20	..	..	..	8 48	9 0	....	..	..	10 20	10 56	....
Brixton Road *Stockwell Road*	..	4 37	6 10	6 30	..	..	..	8 57	9 9	....	..	..	10 30	11 6	....
Clapham Common Stn., *Underground*	4 39	4 46	6 21	6 41	..	..	..	9 6	9 18	....	..	..	10 41	11 17	....
Clapham Junction	X4 44	4 56	6 31	6 51	..	..	..	9 15	9 27	....	..	..	10 51	..	....
CHELSEA *Kings Road*	..	5 6	6 43	7 3	..	..	..	9 24	9 36	....	..	..	11 3	..	....

SO–Saturday only.   SO–Sunday only.   SX–Saturday excepted.   X–Time at Battersea *Queenstown Road.*
†–Time at Clapham Common *Long Road.*   *–Early Journey.

EARLIER JOURNEYS–SUNDAY

Chelsea to Clapham Common at 6 53 a.m.
Chelsea to Brixton at 7 16 a.m.
Chelsea to Clapham Junction at 7 41 a.m.
Chelsea to Blackfriars at 8 1 a.m.
Chelsea to Stockwell at 8 22 a.m.
Clapham Common to Brixton at 6 29 a.m.
Clapham Common to Camberwell at 7 1, 7 52, 8 19, 8 28 a.m.
Clapham Junction to Clapham Common at 7 53 a.m.

Clapham Common to Chelsea at 6 29, 7 18 a.m.
Clapham Common to Clapham Junction at 8 8, 8 20, 8 35 a.m.
Camberwell to Clapham Junction at 7 23, 8 39 a.m.
Camberwell to Chelsea at 8 12 a.m.
Brixton to Chelsea at 7 48, 7 48 a.m.
Stockwell to Chelsea at 8 47 a.m.
Clapham Junction to Chelsea at 7 51 a.m.

17. A variety of personal and public transport is arrayed before the photographer in this September 1950 view of Battersea Bridge Road. Car 192 heads for the terminus whilst an RTL type motor bus lurks in the background. The latter vehicle is a harbinger of doom for the tramcars. (J.H.Meredith)

18. The signs indicate that Battersea Bridge is closed to all other traffic. In March 1950 a collier, the "John Hopkinson" struck and badly damaged one of the piers of the bridge. Car 1397, pictured here just a short distance from the new "enforced" terminus, was partly reconditioned by LT in 1934 and this accounts for the flush sides and other improvements such as the driver's windscreen and the Ashanco ventilators at the top end corner of the lower saloon.   (D.Trevor Rowe)

19. Just north of the temporary terminus was a spur track leading to the former LCC permanent way yard at Battersea Wharf. This site was used for the distribution of the dried sand carried by every service car as an aid to adhesion. The yard was closed in December 1928, but as can be seen, the connecting rails survived. (W.A.Camwell)

1933 map Battersea Bridge and the
LCC permanent way yard.

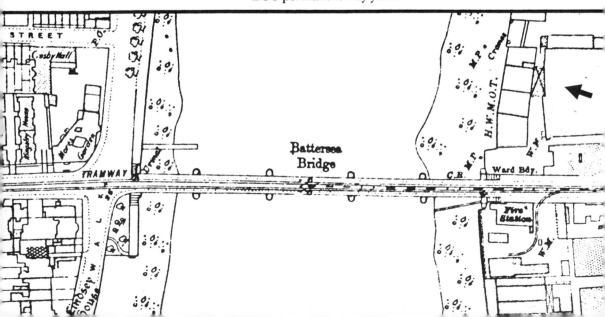

20. We look towards the damaged bridge and the abandoned tramlines over the Thames. (D.Jones Coll.)

21. It is 15th March 1949 and car 1797 rumbles across Battersea Bridge, followed by a well laden mechanical horse. (D.A.Thompson)

22. Car 1 crests the bridge on an enthusiasts tour in July 1949. This prototype car is now to be found at the National Tramway Museum at Crich in Derbyshire. South London spreads out in front of the tram; those were the days when the perspective was strictly "low rise" with no tower blocks in sight. (J.H.Meredith)

23. Battersea Bridge was designed by that emminent victorian, Sir Joseph Bazalgette, and was opened on 31st July 1890. The roadway, which later contained these "gutter running" conduit tram tracks, was 24ft./7 metres wide. Car 1798 approaches the traffic lights at the junction of Cheyne Walk on the Chelsea side of the river. (H.B.Priestley)

24. "A tram for all seasons"...springtime comes to Beaufort Street. Car 1919 occupies the single track stub at the end of the line. Kings Road crosses behind the tram and to the right are some of the artisan dwellings erected on the site of property formerly owned by that great Englishman, Sir Thomas More. (D.A.Thompson)

Flying Bombs   3475

As you will have seen from the Home Secretary's statement in Parliament recently, a system of local warnings will shortly be provided to give notice of imminent danger from flying bombs.

The amount of warning given cannot be more than about a minute and a half. The warning signal, which will be known as the " Danger Warning," will be three two-second blasts on a klaxon or other suitable instrument. The signal to indicate that the danger had passed, which will be known as the " Release," will be a continuous blast lasting six seconds.

On hearing the imminent danger signal, drivers should stop their vehicles at once and passengers be given the opportunity of leaving the vehicle. It has been agreed with the Transport and General Workers' Union that, having regard to the importance of keeping the services running, drivers and conductors should act on their own initiative in taking cover during imminent danger warnings, but that immediately the " Release " is sounded vehicles must proceed on their journeys. All uniformed officials will continue to act as " Spotters " during alerts.

When the " Release " is sounded passengers should be permitted to board the first available vehicle and tickets must be accepted.

25. Pictured in the summer sunshine towards the end of the Second World War, car 1779 stands at the terminus. This was the nearest the trams got to the fashionable quarters of Chelsea and the West End. All the LCC's extension plans were turned down by a powerful anti-tram lobby of residents and vested interests. In this seemingly peaceful scene, it is easy to forget the horrors of the blitz and the then ever present threat of flying bombs. With a cheerful fatalism, so characteristic of the species, many Londoners preferred to travel by tram because the noise inside the car masked the sound of air raids. (V.E.Burrows)

LT circular issued in September 1944.

BATTERSEA, PRINCES
HEAD TO FALCON ROAD

26. The bridge carrying the West London Extension Railway crosses Battersea Park Road at its western end near Christ Church. The terminal loop wires for trolleybus 612 lead off into Candahar Road. (J.H.Meredith)

27. By the combined trolleybus and tram stop there is time for the conductor to have a chat with the lady standing in the roadway. Note the war scarred ruins on the left. (R.J.Harley Coll.)

28. We pull back a little from the previous view to observe a service 12 vehicle by the side of its pre-war, part replacement 612 trolleybus. In this feast of electric traction we also encounter car 1884, a powerful, four motor car of class HR2, more at home tackling the hills of Dulwich than the comparatively gentle gradients of Battersea Park Road. (J.H.Meredith)

LT timetable for service 31, December 1943. Note the all night service which was given the number 3 from 19th June 1946.

ROUTE **31**	**Battersea - Vauxhall - Westminster - Bloomsbury**	P.M. times are
ALL NIGHT ROUTE	**Battersea - Vauxhall - Westminster - Blackfriars**	in heavy figures

Via Battersea Park Road, Nine Elms Lane, Wandsworth Road, Albert Embankment, Lambeth Palace Road, Westminster Bridge, Victoria Embankment, Kingsway Subway, Southampton Row, Theobalds Road.
RAILWAY STATIONS SERVED : Battersea Park, Vauxhall, Westminster, Charing Cross, Holborn.
Service interval : WEEKDAYS 8 mins. (peak hours 6 mins., evening 12 mins.). SUNDAY 12 mins. (evening 15 mins.). No service, Mon. to Fri. normal hours, Sat. aft. and all day Sunday between Bloomsbury and Scotland Yard

	MON. to FRI.		SATURDAY		SUNDAY		ALL NIGHT SERVICE						
	First	Last	First	Last	First	Last	Sat. night, Sun. morn. excepted						
BATTERSEA *Princes Head*	5 59	6 43	10 37	5 59	2 8	10 37	7 40	10 37	....	1 1	2 3	3 3	4 3	....
Vauxhall *Station, SR*	6 16	7 0	10 54	6 16	2 25	10 54	7 55	10 54	11 57	1 16	2 18	3 18	4 18	..
Westminster *Scotland Yard*	6 25	7 9	11 3	6 25	2 34	11 3	8 3	11 3	12 8	1 27	2 27	3 27	4 27	..
Blackfriars *John Carpenter Street*	..	..	..	..	..	..	....	..	12 13	1 32	2 32	3 32	4 32	..
Embankment *Waterloo Bridge*	6 29	7 13	..	6 29	2 36	..	....	..	....	..	..	..	..	..
BLOOMSBURY *Southampton Row*	6 32	7 16	..	6 32	2 39	..	....	..	....	..	..	..	..	..
BLOOMSBURY *Southampton Row*	5 26	6 12	..	5 26	2 28	..	....	..	....	..	..	..	..	..
Embankment *Waterloo Bridge*	5 29	6 15	..	5 29	2 31	..	....	..	....	..	..	..	..	..
Blackfriars *John Carpenter Street*	..	..	..	..	..	..	..	..	12 14	1 33	2 33	3 33	4 33	..
Westminster *Scotland Yard*	5 33	6 19	10 8	5 33	2 33	10 8	7 12	10 8	12 19	1 38	2 38	3 38	4 38	..
Vauxhall *Station, SR*	5 42	6 28	10 17	5 42	2 42	10 17	7 21	10 17	12 30	1 47	2 47	3 47	4 47	..
BATTERSEA *Princes Head*	5 58	6 46	10 35	5 58	2 59	10 35	7 39	10 35	12 48	2 2	3 2	4 2	5 2	..

Service on Weekdays between Battersea and Bloomsbury during the following periods only :
Battersea to Bloomsbury, MON. to FRI., 5 59 to 9 10, 9 50 a.m., 3 5 to 6 43, 9 19, 9 32, 9 51, 10 1, 10 37 p.m. ; SAT.
5 59 to 2 8, 2 22, 2 40, 2 54, 7 5, 9 19, 9 32, 9 51, 10 1, 10 37 p.m.
Bloomsbury to Battersea, MON. to FRI., 5 26 to 9 24 a.m., 3 25 to 6 12 p.m. ; SAT., 5 26 to 2 28 p.m.
Continuous service between Battersea and Westminster *Scotland Yard.*
*—Later journeys, Battersea to Bloomsbury, SUNDAY at 9 13, 9 29, 10 1, 10 37 p.m.
†—Earlier journeys, Bloomsbury to Battersea, SUNDAY at 7 5, 7 21, 7 34, 7 46 a.m.

29. Unkind critics of South London sometimes allude to the climate as one of its detracting factors. This photo proves that even in the rain soaked streets near the Princes Head one could detect a melancholy charm. The reflection of a service 31 car provides a rather haunting image of years gone by. (R.J.S.Wiseman)

30. On our arrival at Princes Head we meet up with "odd man out" car 160, the only E3 class tram not fitted with trolley poles. This hardly mattered on service 31 as the line traversed streets only equipped with conduit tramways. In this 1937 view, car 160 is about to reverse for the journey across London via the Kingsway Subway to Hackney. In December 1939, because of the trolleybus conversions in North London, this service was cut back to run from Islington Green to the Princes Head. (K.H.Rudolph)

34

BLACKFRIARS
VIA CAMBERWELL

TEA

167

31. A sign of things to come as a brand new trolleybus passes the end of Winders Road. Official LT policy favoured the gradual replacement of all the capital's tramways and it was considered only a matter of time before service 31 would also fall to the trolleybus. However, a certain German dictator and his air force had other more explosive ideas to contribute to the metropolitan transport strategy. After the war it was felt that the less "wirebound" the better and all the remaining tram routes succumbed to the diesel bus. (K.H.Rudolph)

32. We are looking east, both literally and metaphorically, as we note car 167 flanked by a motor bus and a trolleybus on the terminal stand in Cabul Road. Many of the streets in this area were named in honour of fomer Battersea resident Sir George Pollock, who rose to the rank of Field Marshal after his exploits in Afghanistan and India. (Tramway Museum Society)

1920 map of Battersea Princes Head area.

33. The tracks in the foreground curve into Falcon Road as car 1962 is about to depart straight ahead for Wandsworth. Service 31 was subject to a lot of chopping and changing during the war years and it only received its final form in October 1947 when it was extended to run from Wandsworth High Street. In the background note the 612 trolleybus parked on the "wrong" side of Cabul Road. This was a very odd terminal stand; Daimler no. D108, GYL 273, pulls over to the lefthand kerb in the more usual manner. (W.A.Camwell)

34. The embodiment of the philosophy "its never too late to learn" is witnessed here as car 1812 is spotted on driver training duties. It would be unfair to venture an opinion as to the cause of the badly dented dash on a vehicle bearing L plates! This is Falcon Road, a week before the end of tram service 34 which normally used these tracks. (J.H.Meredith)

35. Caught on film in the summer of 1950 at Cornell's Corner, car 167 ekes out the last months of service 34 before its transformation into bus route 45. (D.A.Thompson)

36. Car 194 proceeds northwards along Falcon Road towards the gloom of a series of railway bridges which carry tracks to Clapham Junction Station. The trolleybus wires on this stretch were attached to wooden channels under the bridge for over 100 yards/92 metres. This imposed a 5mph/8kmh speed limit at this point on buses working routes 626, 628 and 655 which terminated on the other side of the bridge in Grant Road. The last trolleybus operated here on 8th November 1960. (J.H.Meredith)

CLAPHAM JUNCTION TO EAST HILL, WANDSWORTH

37. A tram swings across from Lavender Hill into Falcon Road. Note the disused west to north curves redundant since the trolleybus conversion of 1937. Note also the wealth of street furniture gathered on the traffic island to the right of the tram. As well as the public convenience, the site includes several trolleybus traction standards, a section box with telephone, a group of public telephone boxes, a traffic light, a street lamp and an array of notices on a board. (J.H.Meredith)

38. Tram meets trolleybus at Clapham Junction in June 1949. The conductor peers out from car 598 which shows KINGS RD CHELSEA on the indicator blind. The 655 trolleybus has an altogether longer haul to reach Acton Vale via Putney and Hammersmith. (J.H.Meredith)

39. A fine aerial view of the junction includes an LCC double deck car on its way to the terminus in East Hill. A single deck tram can just be glimpsed at the terminus of service 34 which at that time ran from Clapham Junction to Kings Road, Chelsea. In June 1915 a north to east connection was installed and the 34s were extended to Waterloo Station via Clapham, Stockwell and Kennington. (J.H.Price Coll.)

40. The nightmare of motor traffic in towns was well in the future when this picture was taken of the old horse tram depot by the footpath leading to Clapham Junction Station. Pasted to the edge of the roof is a notice advertising 900 tram horses for sale, casualties of the electric revolution. (Lens of Sutton)

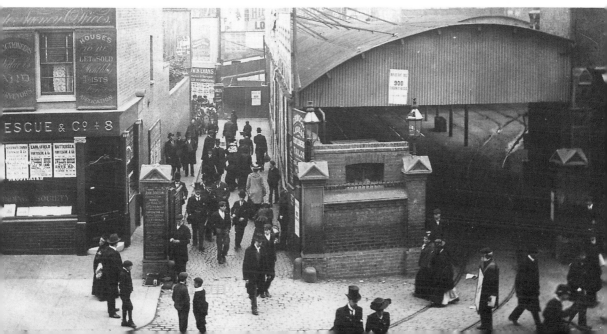

Clapham Junction.

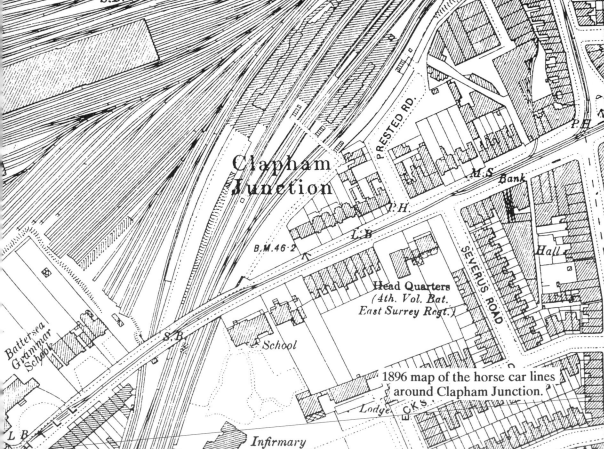

Clapham Junction

1896 map of the horse car lines around Clapham Junction.

41. We return to ground level at Clapham Junction to look from St.John's Hill to Lavender Hill. On the right of the picture is the well known local store, Arding and Hobbs; on the left is the entrance to the former horse car depot. (Lens of Sutton)

42. In July 1949 a newly repainted car 1803 stands next to rehabilitated car 1775. This latter tram was partly modernised in November 1936 and a similar vehicle is now in the final stages of restoration at the National Tramway Museum in Crich, Derbyshire. (A.B.Cross)

43. The end of the line for service 26 from September 1937 was this crossover on St.John's Hill. Trolleybus 626 then took over the section from here to Hammersmith and beyond; the truncated service 26 was later replaced by bus route 168 from 1st October 1950. (H.B.Priestley)

44. "Wiv a ladder and some glasses, You could see to 'Ackney Marshes, If it wasn't for the 'ouses in between." So ran the refrain of a turn of the century song performed by Gus Elen, the famous London music hall artiste. Many of the passengers on this LCC horse tram would have been familiar with these verses. The tramways had contributed to the urbanisation of London, a process which was accelerated by the conversion to electric operation. This allowed folk to live some distance from their place of work. The tram here is pictured on the loop outside Battersea Grammar School in St.John's Hill. (G.Druce Coll.)

ROUTE No. 30.
Waterloo Station to East Hill (Electric Traction).

1. Royal Waterloo Hospital.
2. Union Jack Club.
3. Royal Victoria Hall.
4. Morley College.
5. Surrey Vaudeville.
6. Borough Polytechnic.
7. South London Music Hall.
8. Metropolitan Tabernacle.
9. Kennington Theatre.
10. Kennington Oval.
11. South Western Fever Hospital.
12. Clapham Church.
13. Shakespeare Theatre.
14. New Grand Theatre of Varieties.
15. Freemasons' Orphan School.
16. Royal Victoria Patriotic School.

WATERLOO STATN.
WATERLOO RD.
BLACKFRIARS ROAD
To Hop Exchange.
To Victoria Embankt.
WESTMINSTER BRIDGE RD.
BOROUGH RD.
LONDON RD.
NEWINGTON CAUSEWAY
To St. George's Ch. & Southwark Bridge.
To Tower Bridge.
New X. to St. George's Ch. & Southwark Bridge.
New X. Catford, Greenwich, Blackwall, Brockley & Forest Hill.
NEW KENT RD.
LAMBETH RD.
St. GEORGES ROAD
NEWINGTON BUTTS
To Victoria Embankt.
To Battersea, Tooting Junc. &
ELEPHANT & CASTLE
To Camberwell, Peckham, New X., Lee Green, Forest Hill, Peckham Rye, Loughborough Junction & Brixton, Herne Hill, Norwood.
WALWORTH ROAD
To Westminster & Victoria Embankt.
KENNINGTON ROAD
KENNINGTON PK. RD.
NEW ST.
KENNINGTON PARK
KENNINGTON GATE
To Camberwell, Peckham, New X., Woolwich, Catford & Forest Hill.
HARLEYFORD ST.
To Vauxhall & Victoria.
CAMBERWELL NEW ROAD
BRIXTON RD.
To Streatham, Norbury, Mitcham, Tooting.
DORSET RD.
To Vauxhall & Victoria.
LAMBETH ROAD
CLAPHAM ROAD
STOCKWELL RD.
To Brixton, Streatham, Norbury, Loughboro' Junc., Herne Hill & Norwood.
"THE SWAN"
CLAPHAM ROAD STATN.
THE PLOUGH
To Chelsea Bridge.
To Vauxhall, Victoria & Hop Exchange.
QUEENS RD.
WANDSWORTH RD.
CEDARS RD.
TOWN HALL
LAVENDER HILL
LONG ROAD
NORTH SIDE
HIGH ST.
CLAPHAM COMN.
CLAPHAM COMMON
To Balham, Tooting & Merton.
To Battersea, Fulham, Vauxhall, Westminster Embankment, Blackfriars & Hop Exchange.
FALCON RD.
CLAPHAM JUNCTION
PLOUGH ROAD
St. JOHN'S HILL

LCC route diagram from the
1911 Tramways Guide

45. East Hill, as it once appeared, before it was carved up by the Trinity Road underpass. Those readers interested in request stops like the one fixed to the gas lamp, should consult companion album *Victoria and Lambeth* *Tramways* for a fuller description. Just past the stop, a car on service 28 approaches the terminus situated by the tram in the distance. (J.H.Price Coll.)

46. On 15th December 1909 the first fare paying passengers disembarked from the new electric trams outside the Wandsworth Town Hall. This postcard view dates from circa 1913, and car 512 is seen working service 30 to Waterloo Station. This service was omitted from the October 1915 tramways map and guide; it is likely that it ceased in June when service 34 was extended. (J.H.Price Coll.)

47. A final look at the East Hill terminus reveals car 17 standing opposite the entrance to Alma Road. The link to Wandsworth High Street was later constructed by the firm of W.Manders. Tracks were laid the 414 yards/ 378 metres to a new junction with existing lines in York Road and Garratt Lane. The whole job cost £64,279 and the section opened on 4th August 1921. (J.H.Price Coll.)

LAVENDER HILL

48. Car 1833, its indicator blind already showing VICTORIA for the return journey, stops outside Arding and Hobbs. Lavender Hill looks pleasantly empty in the sunshine, and the tramtracks stretch away inviting us to explore further. (A.B.Cross)

49. In the lower left hand corner is the connecting curve from Falcon Road used by service 34 cars. In the distance, on the London side of the approaching tramcar, is Battersea Public Library built in 1890 to a neo-Dutch style. (H.B.Priestley)

50. A two tram line up waits for the lights on Lavender Hill at the junction with Latchmere Road. Cars 1771 and 163, although bearing a strong family resemblance, neatly illustrate the differences in destination equipment and windscreen style to be found in the post-war fleet. (J.H.Meredith)

51. This service 26 tram is returning to Clapham Depot after the morning peak and has been caught by the camera at the Latchmere Road crossover on Lavender Hill. From the summer of 1949 many of the Wandsworth Depot duties were taken over by Clapham so that space could be released for bus conversion works. (J.H.Meredith)

Via Lavender Hill, Wandsworth Road, Vauxhall Cross, Albert Embankment, Lambeth Palace Road, Westminster Bridge, Victoria Embankment, Blackfriars Bridge, Southwark Street

RAILWAY STATIONS SERVED : Clapham Junction, Wandsworth Road, Vauxhall, Westminster, Charing Cross, Temple, Blackfriars, London Bridge

Service interval : WEEKDAYS 7½ minutes (peak hours 5 mins., evening 15 mins.), SUNDAY 12 mins. (evening 14 minutes)

	WEEKDAYS First	WEEKDAYS Last	SUNDAY First		SUNDAY Last				WEEKDAYS First	WEEKDAYS Last	SUNDAY First	SUNDAY Last	
CLAPHAM JUNCTION *Falcon*	5 11	9 46	....	5 57	8 7	10 2	....	LONDON BRIDGE *Borough*	5 56	10 29	§		....
Vauxhall *Station*	5 30	10 4	...	6 11	8 21	10 20	..	Blackfriars Bridge	6 3	10 36	6 29	....	..
Savoy Street *Embankment*	5 44	10 18		6 25	8 33	10 34		Savoy Street *Embankment*	6 5	10 38	6 31	8 35	10 38
Blackfriars Bridge	5 46	10 20		6 27	..	..	..	Vauxhall *Station*	6 20	10 52	6 45	8 47	10 52
LONDON BRIDGE *Borough*	5 54	10 27	....	....	..	..	..	CLAPHAM JUNCTION *Falcon*	6 39	11 10	6 59	9 1	11 10

SPECIAL JOURNEYS

Battersea *Princes Head* to Blackfriars via Battersea, WEEKDAYS at 4 23, 5 0, 5 12, 5 20, 5 45 a.m. ; MONDAY to FRIDAY at 3 45, 4 7, 4 22 p.m. ; SATURDAY at 11 23, 11 54 a.m., 12 19 p.m.

Blackfriars to Battersea *Princes Head*, WEEKDAYS at 4 56, 5 31, 5 44, 5 54 a.m. ; MONDAY to FRIDAY at 8 13, 8 56, 9 13, 9 30 a.m. ; SATURDAY at 8 33, 8 53, 8 56, 9 2, 9 13, 9 30 a.m.

*–Journeys only at 5 57, 6 9, 6 21, 6 33, 6 45, 7 2, 7 14, 7 26, 7 38, 7 50 a.m.   §–Journeys only at 6 29, 6 41, 6 53, 7 5, 7 17, 7 34, 7 46, 7 58, 8 10, 8 22 a.m.

ALL NIGHT ROUTE	Clapham Junction - Vauxhall - Westminster *Stn.* - London Bridge

SATURDAY NIGHT, SUNDAY MORNING EXCEPTED

CLAPHAM JUNCTION *Falcon*	1 7	1 59	2 50	3 45	4 39	4 52	....	LONDON BRIDGE *Borough*		1 33	2 24	3 17	4 12		5 31
Battersea *Queenstown Road*	1 12	2 4	2 55	3 50	4 44	4 57	..	Westminster *Station*	1 42	2 33	3 26	4 21		5 52
Vauxhall *Station*	1 22	2 14	3 5	4 0		5 9	..	Vauxhall *Station*	1 42	2 33	3 26	4 21		5 52
Westminster *Station*	1 31	2 23	3 14	4 9	..	..	Battersea *Queenstown Road*	1 52	2 43	3 36	4 31	4 45	6 4
LONDON BRIDGE *Borough*		....			..	5 30	....	CLAPHAM JUNCTION *Falcon*	1 57	2 48	3 41	4 36	4 50	6 9

52. Battersea Town Hall was designed by a Mr. Mountford who was also responsible for the somewhat grander edifice of the Old Bailey in London. This centre of Battersea civic pride opened in 1893, some eleven years after the horse tramway which ran outside. This view dates from around the inauguration of the electric trams in October 1909.

Town Hall & Shakespere Theatre, Battersea.

53. It seems from this angle that car 348 has a slight tilt as it passes the end of Sugden Road. Above the indicator blind are the three coloured lights which were illuminated at night to help intending passengers find the correct service. This method was used by the LCC before the introduction of large stencils showing service numbers. The East Hill to Victoria service would have shown RED-RED-BLANK, and the East Hill to Hop Exchange via Westminster, BLANK-RED-GREEN. (J.H.Price Coll.)

54. We look east from The Craven public house at the corner of Taybridge Road. In the distance, very close to the junction of Queen's Road and Cedars Road, a tram passes the double kerb of the pavement which indicates that the highway had to be levelled at this spot. In fact, most of this part of Lavender Hill was cut into the original slope of the land which rises to the right of the picture.
(Lens of Sutton)

LONDON. Lavender Hill, Battersea. No. 1795.

55. This is a "before" view with the bakers shop intact behind car 177 which is turning into Cedars Road. Another vehicle of note is the van from Silverthorne Road where the main victualling depot of the Pullman Car Co. was situated. The van is painted in full Pullman livery. (J.H.Meredith)

56. The hill in Cedars Road was the cause of several unfortunate occurences for the trams. In the early days, LCC car 478 had disgraced itself on the slope, thereby narrowly missing a single deck car standing in Queen's Road. The damage shown here was done on 23rd August 1950 by car 1396. The driver lost control of his tram, it then derailed on the curve leading to Lavender Hill and crashed into the front of the shop on the right. The motorman was trapped in the wreckage and two passengers were injured. Car 1396 never ran again. (A.B.Cross)

Many of the older residents of Wandsworth and Battersea have fond memories of the trams; they recall the cheap fares, the all night cars and the frequent services. Another topic of conversation is the "runaway tram" which looms large in local folklore. The tale centres on several accidents caused by rogue tramcars which careered down Cedars Road only to end up embedded in the unfortunate bakers shop on the corner opposite. Of course some of these stories grow in the telling, because the trams in London generally had a good safety record and there was always the lifeguard (called the "cowcatcher" in the vernacular) to scoop up any unfortunate pedestrians who strayed into the path of an oncoming tram. However, the demolition of Hemmings the Bakers caught the imagination and the next few photos illustrate perhaps the most infamous junction on the London system.

Plan of the Cedars Road/Lavender Hill junction.

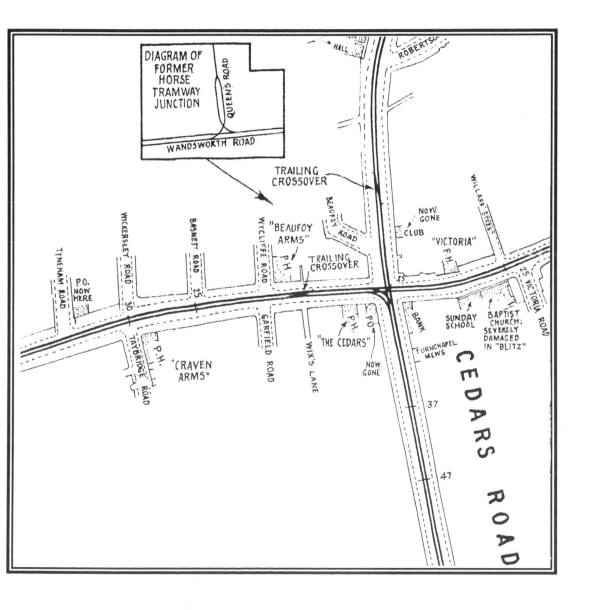

57. One month after the Cedars Road debacle and it is "business as usual" for Hemmings, albeit in temporary accommodation round the corner. (J.H.Meredith)

58. Car 1778 clatters across the junction from Wandsworth Road. Until 1937, service 32 cars passed straight across from Cedars Road to Queen's Road. The date of this photograph is 2nd September 1950 and at the end of the month the tracks will fall silent for ever. No more would the assistants in the bakers shop wince at the sound of a 34 tram descending the hill! (D.A.Thompson)

CEDARS ROAD TO
WANDSWORTH ROAD

59. The gradient in Cedars Road was too severe for horse cars and only electric traction could cope as this view of car 161 demonstrates. The section was opened on 26th February 1910 and it was an official requirement that motormen had to have at least six months experience before being allowed on this hill. (D.A.Thompson)

60. Car 593 halts at the top of Cedars Road before turning into Clapham Common, North Side. This tram is one of series 552-60 cars built by the LCC and described in companion album *Hampstead and Highgate Tramways*. (N.N.Forbes)

61. This pre-First World War look at the entrance to Cedars Road gives a better impression of the drop towards Battersea behind the tramcar. Note the imposing architecture... Victorian gothic at its gloomiest! (J.H.Price Coll.)

62. We now return to Wandsworth Road where we encounter car 317 near Milford Street. (J.H.Price Coll.)

63. By Brayburne Avenue car 1771 halts to set down a passenger. In the background is the railway bridge at Wandsworth Road Station. Other excellent pictures of this location are featured in *South London Line*, one of the London Suburban Railway series by Middleton Press. (D.A.Thompson)

64. The dip under the railway bridge is clearly
visible in this photograph. This was necessary
to allow passage of top covered trams such as
car 1771 which is seen emerging on the London
side by the Lord Raglan public house.
(D.A.Thompson)

ROUTE 28	Clapham Junction - Vauxhall - Victoria	P.M. times an in heavy fig

Via Lavender Hill, Wandsworth Road, Vauxhall Cross, Vauxhall Bridge Road

RAILWAY STATIONS SERVED : Clapham Junction, Wandsworth Road, Vauxhall, Victoria

Service interval : WEEKDAYS 7½ mins. (peak hours 5 mins., evening 15 mins.) ; SUNDAY 12 mins. (evening 15 mins.)

	WEEKDAYS		SUNDAY				WEEKDAYS		SUNDAY	
	First	Last	First	Last			First	Last	First	Last
CLAPHAM JUNCTION Falcon	5 35	9 45	7 58	9 45		VICTORIA Clock Tower	6 3	10 20	8 22	10 20
Vauxhall Station	5 54	10 3	8 12	10 3		Vauxhall Station	6 11	10 28	8 28	10 28
VICTORIA Clock Tower	6 2	10 11	8 18	10 11		CLAPHAM JUNCTION Falcon	6 30	10 46	8 42	10 46

LT timetable for service 28, December 1943

65. At the crossover by Miles Street car 1809 approaches the junction with Nine Elms Lane. A short way ahead lies the busy tramway layout at Vauxhall which is fully described in *Victoria and Lambeth Tramways*. (J.H.Meredith)

66. Just west of the Princes Head was this stretch of single track in York Road. The motorman of the service 12 tram must keep an eye on the cyclist who seems intent on squeezing through the gap by the parked Austin van. Most bike riders of this era would use their common sense and approach tramlines with caution, especially when the surrounding granite setts were wet and slippery. (J.C.Gillham)

67. It could be a sobering experience for an unwary motorist when 16 tons of tramcar suddenly swung from single to double track as we see here in York Road. Luckily most Londoners with motor cars were well used to these antics. On the credit side, the tramtracks did impose lane discipline on motorists, which in modern times is conspicuous by its absence. (D.Trevor Rowe)

68. Car 209 is about to regain the double track after passing along this single line equipped with double conduit slots. The lorry parked on the left serves to accentuate the narrowness of this part of York Road. (D.Jones Coll.)

69. At the corner of Totteridge Road car 1762 slows for the facing points at the end of the single track. The motorman may have been intent on keeping ahead of his trackless rival looming up in the background.
(J.H.Meredith)

70. This part of Battersea by the Creek Road crossover once boasted various factories, engineering works and saw mills. Many of these establishments had direct wharf access to the Thames. The tracks in the centre of the picture are set wider apart but the opportunity has been lost to provide suitable loading islands for tram passengers. (J.H.Meredith)

ROUTE 12	Wandsworth - Battersea - Vauxhall - London Bridge			P.M. times are in heavy figures

Via York Road, Battersea Park Road, Nine Elms Lane, Wandsworth Road, Albert Embankment, Lambeth Road, Borough Road, Southwark Bridge Road, Southwark Street

RAILWAY STATIONS SERVED : Wandsworth Town, Battersea Park, Vauxhall, London Bridge

Service interval : MONDAY to FRIDAY 8 mins. (peak hours 5 mins., evening 12 mins.), SATURDAY 6-8 mins. (evening 12 mins.), SUNDAY 13 mins (evening 15 mins.)

	WEEKDAYS First		SUNDAY First	DAILY Last				WEEKDAYS First		SUNDAY First	DAILY Last	
WANDSWORTH High St., York Rd.	*437	5 7	539	9 51	....	LONDON BRIDGE Borough	....		5 20	619	....	10 33	....
Battersea Princes Head	4 44	516	547	10 0	..	Vauxhall Station	....		5 35	6 32	..	10 48	..
Battersea Park Road Queenstown Rd.	4 51	523	554	10 7	..	Battersea Park Road Queenstown Rd.	..		5 47	6 40	..	11 0	..
Vauxhall Station	5 0	532	6 2	1017	..	Battersea Princes Head	..	*5 1	5 53	6 47	..	11 6	..
LONDON BRIDGE Borough	515	547	615	1031	..	WANDSWORTH High St., York Rd.	5 6	6 2	6 55	..	11 15	..

*—Time at Wandsworth London Transport Depot.

SPECIAL EARLY JOURNEYS—SUNDAY

Wandsworth London Transport Depot to John Carpenter Street at 3 52 a.m.
Wandsworth London Transport Depot to Westminster at 5 29 a.m.
Battersea Princes Head to John Carpenter Street at 5 4 a.m.

John Carpenter Street to Battersea Princes Head at 4 32 a.m.
John Carpenter Street to Clapham Junction at 5 36 a.m.
Westminster to Wandsworth High Street at 6 1 a.m.

LT timetable for service 12, December 1943

71. This is basically the same scene as the previous photograph, but from a vantage point on the top deck of an approaching tramcar. The crossover is situated directly beneath the section feed for the 612 trolleybuses. (H.B.Priestley)

72. The film posters outside the Savoy in York Road are being changed as car 205 passes a temporary stop sign. These "dolly" stops used to appear in the transition period between the removal of the old tram stops and the unveiling of the brand new bus versions. (J.H.Meredith)

73. Car 200 is about to make the trip up Jews Row to Wandsworth Depot. The whole of this area has since been transformed by new highways on the southern approach to Wandsworth Bridge. The neat community of terraced houses depicted here has been sacrificed to a bleak, unattractive landscape of fume ridden concrete. (J.H.Meredith)

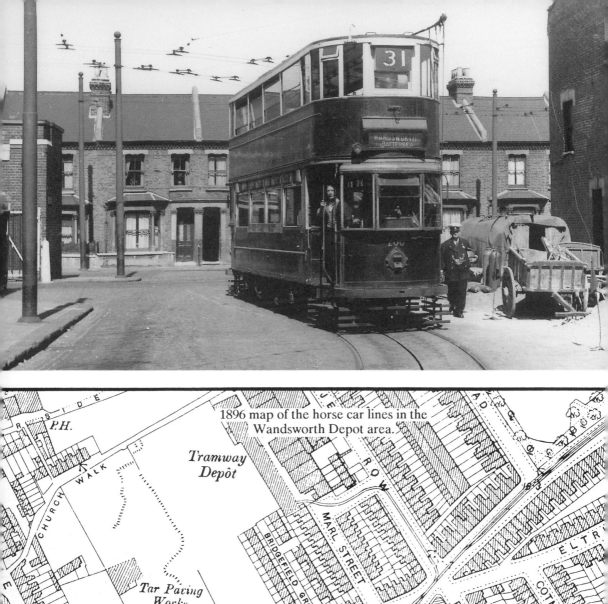

1896 map of the horse car lines in the Wandsworth Depot area.

74. We follow the progress of car 200 which is seen on the connecting curve by the depot entrance. The date is 6th June 1949 and already the contractors' huts and equipment are being unloaded for the imminent building work to convert the depot to bus operation. (J.H.Meredith)

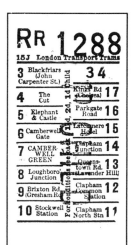

RR 1288		
15J London Transport Trams		
3 Blackfriars (John Carpenter St.)		34
4 The Cut	King's Rd (Chelsea)	17
5 Elephant & Castle	Parkgate Road	16
6 Camberwell Gate	Latchmere Hotel	15
7 CAMBERWELL GREEN	Clapham Junction	14
8 Loughboro' Junction	Queens-town Rd. (Lavender Hill)	13
9 Brixton Rd (Gresham Rd)	Clapham Common Station	12
10 Stockwell Station	Clapham North Stn.	11

For conditions see back 2d, 1d Child

SOUTH LONDON TRAMWAYS CO.	
Wb 3620	
FARE 1d TO OR FROM	Wandsworth Town and 'Prince's Head' Tavern
	Plough Lane and Brighton Railway Stn.
	'Prince's Head' Tavern and 'Rifleman' Tavern.
	Brighton Railway Stn. and Vauxhall Cross.
	'Rifleman' Tavern and Westminster Bridge.

75. If this tram were returned to the same position nowadays, it would be standing somewhere between McDonalds the fast food chain, and a Mercedes Benz dealer. Such have been the changes over the past 45 years that, apart from the depot building which still survives, there are almost no other points of reference left. (H.B.Priestley)

76. On one night in June 1949, a hundred trams had to be moved around seven depots to make space for the builders in Wandsworth and Clapham depots. For safety reasons overhead wiring was erected inside Wandsworth car shed during the conversion period and the conduit rails serving the inspection pits and access tracks were either removed or rendered electrically dead. The rear tram in this picture is already using the temporary overhead whilst the car in the foreground is still working on the conduit. (Lens of Sutton)

77. The photographer has managed to remain inside car 1961 after it has been stabled for the night in the depot. The bulkhead door has been slid open to reveal the controller. This particular car was upholstered in blue moquette. (H.B.Priestley)

78. Wandsworth Depot was constructed on the site of the former horse car sheds situated just off Jews Row. It originally had a capacity of 103 cars stored on 16 roads. In July 1927 the official capacity was listed as 95 cars and by February 1950, after the start of reconstruction, this number had dwindled to 36. In this picture lined up from left to right are an LT "rehab" car, an ex-LCC E3 class car, two ex-West Ham cars employed for non-passenger duties and a 612 trolleybus. Wandsworth shared with Holloway the distinction of operating both trams and trolleybuses during the post-war period. In the foreground one of the two traversers can just be glimpsed. These moving platforms shifted vehicles sideways from one depot road to the next; they were a standard feature in LCC tram depots. (Lens of Sutton)

79. The single track connection to Wandsworth Depot is behind this tram which is positioned just east of the crossover by Warple Way. This location today is now known as Old York Road and Warple Way has vanished together with much housing. A new highway now takes through traffic north of Wandsworth Town Station. (J.H.Meredith)

80. The tram with the photographer on board waits under Wandsworth Town railway bridge for the oncoming car to clear the single track opposite Alma Road. (H.B.Priestley)

81. We look in the other direction to the previous view. Note the double conduit in the foreground and the informative Southern Electric signs placed to entice passengers away from the trams. (J.C.Gillham)

82. The railway bridge offers a splendid panorama of the traffic passing along York Road past the Alma public house. In this scene dated 27th June 1949, we observe a 31 tram about to enter the single track. Just underneath us we are treated to a close up look at the intricacies of trolleybus overhead wiring. (H.B.Priestley)

83. A well earned rest is granted to the members of this track gang as they pause for the moment to be captured on film. Civil engineering was more labour intensive in the first decade of the twentieth century. Manual work of this nature was back breaking; it was only by the efforts of countless unsung heroes that the massive job of building the London County Council Tramways was completed. Similar single track, double conduit layouts existed at Greenwich and Stockwell. (LCC official photo)

84. The horse tramway in Fairfield Road was not converted to electric traction because the new conduit lines were incorporated into an extension of York Road west of North Street to merge with the former Red Lion Street by the Ram Brewery. However, the tracks remained after the last horse car departed in May 1906 and they were used very infrequently by a lone horse tram borrowed from one of the LCC's last equine operations in Rotherhithe (a similar vehicle is featured in picture 67 of *Southwark and Deptford Tramways*). This "ghost tram" lasted until April 1914. (J.H.Price Coll.)

85. Road works associated with the imminent trolleybus conversion are in full swing as car 626 heads for Wandsworth town centre on service 12. The new 612 trolleybus route will shortly take over the section along Garratt Lane towards Tooting and Mitcham. This new overhead wiring installation includes two traction standards planted behind the advert hoarding to the left of the picture. Obviously on conduit tramways London Transport could not replace older tramway poles on a one for one basis, as was the case in other ex-company and municipal areas where the trams had used the conventional overhead system.
(A.B.Cross)

86. These two trams are not far from the terminus in York Road and they are waiting to return to town. Both vehicles will keep each other company until north of Vauxhall when car 1962 will use Lambeth Road to cut across inner South London to arrive at its northern terminus of Hop Exchange. The service 31 car will finish its journey at Westminster on this sunny March day in 1950. (J.H.Meredith)

87. The Salvation Army Citadel on the corner of Shoreham Street presides over a gathering of terminating trams. Unfortunately there was little prospect of salvation for the electric vehicles as their owner, London Transport, was busy laying out a large scrap yard at Penhall Road, Charlton where all the cars in this picture would eventually meet a fiery end. (D.Trevor Rowe)

1910 map of central Wandsworth showing the original electric layout before the extensions from East Hill and Putney Bridge Road.

88. This view was reputedly taken in the summer of 1943. It shows car 1727 with white painted fenders and headlamp mask to conform with strict wartime blackout regulations. The diamond shape on the top deck window indicates that anti-blast netting has been fixed to the glass. The trolleybus traction standards sport a couple of white rings in an attempt to stop other road users colliding with them in the gloom of the blackout. Lack of motor traffic can be ascribed to petrol rationing. The Salvation Army posters on the wall bear witness to the fact that this organisation was one of the key voluntary groups devoted to the welfare of war weary citizens, many of whom had lost everything in the bombing. (V.E.Burrows)

89. The tram in front is about to reverse on the crossover. We look south towards the junction with Garratt Lane in the distance. The lines depicted here were not the first tramway to be laid in this part of York Road, that honour goes to the plateway tracks of the Surrey Iron Railway which passed on the right hand side next to the Ram Brewery. (H.B.Priestley)

90. The name of this thoroughfare has since been altered to Ram Street, although it was still part of York Road when Don Thompson photographed these two trams on 15th March 1949. This picture captures some of the atmosphere portrayed in Norman Collins' book "London belongs to me" published in 1945 and subsequently filmed. In it the author defines something of the essence of the capital..."the Waif and Stray Societies, and the fortune tellers and the pub on the corner and the trams. That's London..."
(D.A.Thompson)

91. Not a tram in sight, but the rails can just be discerned to the left of the 612 trolleybus which is about to pass the Ram Inn and Brewery, headquarters of Young and Company. This site dates back to around 1675 and the buildings still contain two beam engines of 1835 and 1867 vintage respectively. Deliveries of Young's excellent ales are still made to local hostelries by traditional drays drawn by fine shire horses.
(C.Carter)

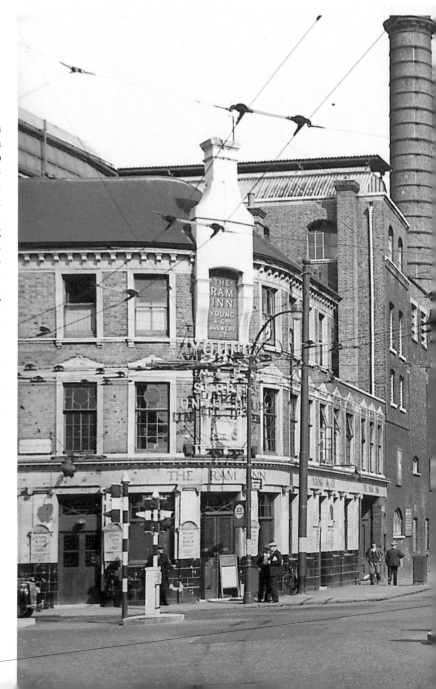

ROUTE No. 29.

Hop Exchange to Tooting Junction and Victoria Embankment (John Carpenter-street) to Summerstown (Electric Traction).

1. City of London School.
2. Sion College.
3. Metropolitan Asylums Board Offices.
4. The Temple.
5. L. C. C. Education Offices.
6. Somerset House.
7. Savoy Theatre.
8. Charing Cross Station.
9. Trafalgar Square.
10. New Scotland Yard.
11. Westminster Abbey.
12. Houses of Parliament.
13. St. Thomas's Hospital.
14. London Bridge Station.

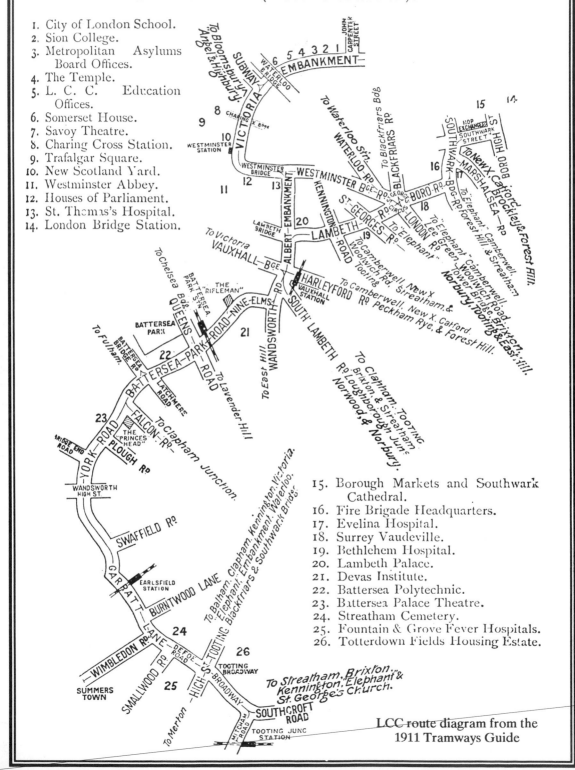

15. Borough Markets and Southwark Cathedral.
16. Fire Brigade Headquarters.
17. Evelina Hospital.
18. Surrey Vaudeville.
19. Bethlehem Hospital.
20. Lambeth Palace.
21. Devas Institute.
22. Battersea Polytechnic.
23. Battersea Palace Theatre.
24. Streatham Cemetery.
25. Fountain & Grove Fever Hospitals.
26. Totterdown Fields Housing Estate.

LCC route diagram from the 1911 Tramways Guide

92. Outside the Ram Inn the colourful spectacle unfolds of LCC car 445 looking very smart in its crimson lake and primrose livery. This postcard view was taken a few days after the electric service opened in August 1906.

The tram is running from Tooting Broadway to Creek Road crossover (illustrated in picture 71). The through route to Central London via Battersea Park Road was inaugurated on 22nd December 1906. (D.Jones Coll.)

93. Cars 428 and 1737 are pictured outside the County Court building in Garratt Lane. The latter car has just arrived from Wandsworth Depot and is about to reverse to follow the service 30 tram. The three line destination box

on car 428 shows that this vehicle is heading to NEAR WILLESDEN JUNCTION, a rather vague location which could be more accurately described as the northern end of Scrubs Lane, Harlesden. (K.H.Rudolph)

94. At the Wandsworth end of Putney Bridge Road we observe the change pit where trams altered their method of current collection from trolley to conduit and vice versa. Here car 493 pulls up; it has been using the newly installed trolleybus overhead. (K.H.Rudolph)

1093.—CHANGEOVERS—OVERHEAD TO CONDUIT.

Notice to Conductors.

Conductors are warned that, in order to avoid risk of danger to passengers boarding and alighting at Changeovers, they should remain on the platform whilst the car is in motion picking up the plough. The car must be at a standstill before the trolley boom is removed from the overhead wire.

1094.—PLOUGHS—BAD CONTACT.

Notice to Drivers and Conductors.

The floor flaps on the rehabilitated cars are fitted with a metal edge. Drivers and conductors are warned that they must not touch the plough or bus-bars with the flap as there is danger of receiving an electric shock.

LT circular issued in July 1936

95. Car 464 is an E class vehicle dating from 1906 and it is seen here in September 1937. An LT trolleybus replacement notice which shows details of the new 628 route, has been pasted to the rocker panel of the car. Note that the top of the gas lamp has been in contact with several errant trolley poles! (K.H.Rudolph)

96. The last picture of our trilogy of change pit views shows the characteristic line of ploughs waiting to be forked under cars heading for Wandsworth High Street. This service 30 tram has a full load on board and it will terminate at Tooting Junction. After 7th December 1933 this service was extended all the way to West Croydon and this section of operations is described in companion Middleton Press album *Croydon's Tramways*.
(G.N.Southerden)

97. On newly laid track car 1426, northbound to Shepherds Bush, sweeps round the corner in Putney Bridge Road. Several passers by and the lad near the centre of the picture stand and stare at the latest mechanical marvel of the age. (R.J.Harley Coll.)

98. The cyclist in the foreground is about to cross from the High Street into Putney Bridge Road. Passengers from this neck of the woods had the choice between the motor bus and the tramcar for their journey to Hammersmith. As we can tell by looking at this scene the competition was pretty intense. (D.Jones Coll.)

HIGH ST PUTNEY

ROUTE No. 1.

Hammersmith to Putney and Harlesden (Electric Traction).

LCC route diagram from the 1911 Tramways Guide

1. Fulham Palace.
2. Grand Theatre.
3. Fulham Workhouse.
4. St. Paul's School.
5. Hammersmith Town Hall.
6. Hammersmith School of Arts and Crafts and Trade School for Girls.
7. Shepherd's Bush Empire.
8. Hammersmith Workhouse.
9. Wormwood Scrubbs Prison.
10. Kensal Green Cemetery and St. Mary's Roman Catholic Cemetery.

For business notices upon this route see pages 183.

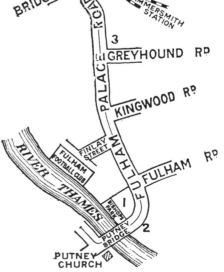

To Harlesden HARROW ROAD To Lock Bridge & Edgware Road.

WILLESDEN JUNCTION

SCRUBBS LANE

WORMWOOD SCRUBBS 9 8

10

ST. QUINTON PARK STN

NORTH POLE RD

WOOD LANE

CORONATION EXHIBITION

WOOD LANE STATION

CENTRAL LONDON RLY

To Ealing, Hanwell, Southall & Uxbridge—UXBRIDGE ROAD 6 7

To Hounslow & Hampton Court. GOLDHAWK ROAD

SHEPHERDS BUSH ROAD

GLENTHORNE RD HAMMERSMITH BROADWAY

To Kew, Hampton Court & Hounslow. KING ST WEST

HAMMERSMITH ROAD 4

HAMMERSMITH STATION

BRIDGE RD

PALACE ROAD

3 GREYHOUND RD

KINGWOOD RD

FULHAM RD

RIVER THAMES

FULHAM FOOTBALL CLUB FINLAY STREET FULHAM

BISHOPS PARK 1

PUTNEY BRIDGE 2

PUTNEY CHURCH

99. Lower Richmond Road, Putney was the original terminus of the electric service from Hammersmith. This location was equipped with a crossover and a trolley reverser, but true to London traditions, most crews preferred to swing the trolley and the "automatic" facility was little used. (D.Jones Coll.)

100. Here we look out across Putney Bridge just in time to glimpse the Cambridge boat engaged in that famous British sporting ritual of the Boat Race. This event brought out the crowds and many spectators would journey here by tramcar. (R.J.Harley Coll.)

101. The River Thames, the grounds of Bishops Park and Fulham Palace make a picturesque setting for a standard LCC tramcar crossing Putney Bridge. This granite structure was opened in 1886 and it replaced an earlier wooden bridge which dated back to 1729. The tramtracks were laid near the kerb and public service began on 23rd January 1909. (J.H.Price Coll.)

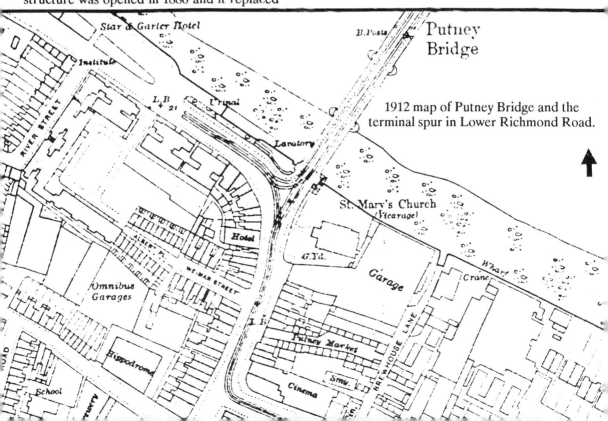

1912 map of Putney Bridge and the terminal spur in Lower Richmond Road.

102. Work began in 1931 on widening Putney Bridge from 44ft./13 metres to 74ft./22 metres; at this stage in the construction pedestrians are already using part of ther new bridge. In the foreground the LCC overhead gang have positioned their tower wagon to assist in the erection of new wiring and traction standards. The permanent way department are not far behind and the alignment of the new tracks can clearly be seen. (R.J.Harley Coll.)

103. Aside from the tram there is an interesting variety of transport on offer in this early 1930s postcard of the widened bridge. At the midpoint of the river crossing lay the boundary between the metropolitan boroughs of Fulham and Wandsworth; this corresponded to the ancient divide between Middlesex on the north bank and Surrey on the Putney side. (J.H.Price Coll.)

104. Numbering of LCC services commenced in 1912 and from then until 1915 the line between Scrubs Lane and Wandsworth High Street was known as service 82. Sometime during this period a tram has been caught on film traversing Fulham Palace Road. These tracks formed a vital north-south connection in the London tramway network. They proved useful in the transfer of rolling stock and many company and municipal cars passed by here in the nocturnal hours. (J.H.Price Coll.)

105. Further along Fulham Palace Road car 999 is passing the corner of Edgarley Terrace on its regular run to Hammersmith Broadway. Construction of this tramway was carried out by the local company of George Wimpey, an enterprise which was later to become one of the world's leading civil engineering firms. (J.H.Price Coll.)

106. The opposition are out in force as a service 28 car passes north of the Finlay Street crossover. (R.J.Harley Coll.)

107. Car 1362 stands with its crew in Great Church Lane, Hammersmith. Tracks to the rear of the tram lead into Hammersmith Depot. This car shed was constructed in stages from 1907 to 1911 and the first part of the building opened in April 1908. The eventual capacity was around 59 cars. Extensive alterations were carried out for the replacing trolleybuses in 1936-37; the building lost its electric vehicles in 1960. In the intervening years the plague of urban redevelopment has infected this area and the whole scene has deteriorated into an appalling mess of elevated highways and ghastly office blocks.
(LCC official photo)

108. Cars 989 and 1576 are loading at Hammersmith Broadway, one of the most important transport interchange points in London. Out of camera shot to the left is the terminus of London United cars serving Brentford, Acton and points west. On the right is the Underground Station; Hammersmith was served by electric trains running on the District and Metropolitan lines from 1905-6. Tube trains belonging to the Great Northern Piccadilly and Brompton Railway were inaugurated by David Lloyd George, then President of the Board of Trade, on 15th December 1906. This precursor of the Piccadilly Line originally operated from Hammersmith to Finsbury Park. (J.H.Price Coll.)

109. It was an expensive business for the LCC to construct connecting lines across Hammersmith Broadway. On 30th January 1912 a single track was opened and full service over double track had to wait until the requisite road widenings had been carried out in May. This picture shows car 448 heading north with the motorman out of uniform. This lends weight to the idea that this view was taken during the troubled days of the 1926 General Strike when "volunteers" tried their hand at tram driving. (D.Jones Coll.)

110. Major "cut and cover" engineering works were necessary when the underground railway tracks were quadrupled at Hammersmith Station in 1930-32. Interruptions to the tram service were minimised by the use of temporary tracks; the service 28 car on the left is about to resume normal running in Queen Caroline Street. The other LCC tram in the picture has just emerged at the end of King Street on the 1922 connecting lines with the London United. (D.Jones Coll.)

111. Our final view shows car 997 heading towards Brook Green and Harlesden. The wiring here has been altered by London Transport for the imminent introduction of trolleybuses. (K.H.Rudolph)

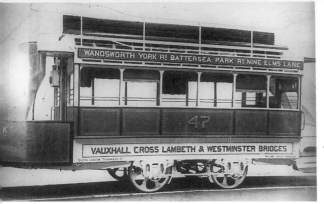

ROLLING STOCK

Class D

Cars 302-376, 377-401. These trams were delivered to the London County Council in 1904. Their basic design was similar to the Class A cars described in *Southwark and Deptford Tramways*. The Brush Company of Loughborough built cars 302-376, whilst the second batch was constructed by the British Electric Car Co. of Trafford Park, Manchester. Electrical equipment was supplied by British Westinghouse and each car rode on a pair of McGuire maximum traction trucks. These vehicles were originally intended for conduit only lines and therefore a plough carrier was fitted to one of the trucks. Seating was for 28 inside and 38 on the upper deck where there was no provision for a trolley standard.

Car 310 was fitted with an experimental top cover in 1904 and this programme was subsequently extended to the rest of the class. Between 1904 and 1914 all D class cars had been altered to include fully enclosed top decks and direct stairs in place of the reversed staircase which restricted the motorman's field of vision. The various sub divisions of this class before 1914 are listed opposite.

112. South London Tramways Company car 47 is seen in original state on delivery from the Lancaster Wagon Company in 1881. Note the knifeboard seating on the top deck; decency panels have yet to be fitted. Each of these vehicles was licensed to carry 42 passengers and the "motive power" was supplied by two horses. On both St.John's Hill and Lavender Hill an extra or "chain" horse was added to the team to ease the burden. This particular car was painted blue and worked on the North Street, Wandsworth to Westminster service. (Lancaster Wagon Co. official photo)

113. This tram is marked CLASS D1 just beneath the name of the Tramways Manager on the right of the rocker panel. Although the top deck balconies offered a splendid ride in fine weather they weren't too practical at other times. Another rather suspect feature was the reversed staircase which was drilled with a number of awkwardly placed peep holes for the driver. A better field of vision was guaranteed by normal direct stairs and these became standard for the LCC fleet. (LCC official photo)

114. Car 315, was officially delicensed on 7th November 1931. It bears the standard LCC livery of purple lake (which had weathered to a deep chocolate brown colour by the time of this photo) and primrose. Note the fully enclosed top deck and the direct stairs. (R.Elliott)

D1. Balcony top covers and reversed stairs.
D2. Enclosed top covers and reversed stairs.
D3. Enclosed top covers and direct stairs.
D4. Open top, direct stairs. Cars equipped with trolley standards.

Only four trams were classified D4 and they worked on the isolated Woolwich to Abbey Wood section; they were replaced by cars of classes M and E1 in 1910/11. Vehicles of class D were associated with New Cross and Wandsworth car sheds and trams at the former depot received trolley poles to operate on through services from the suburbs. Withdrawal of this class was effected in 1929-31; the trucks and electrical equipment were removed by the LCC and the bodies were sold as sheds or caravans.

LONDON COUNTY COUNCIL TRAMCAR

| TYPE: CLASS D | SCALE: |
| CAR Nos. 302 -376 | 4 mm = 1 Foot |

DRAWING No. TC 68

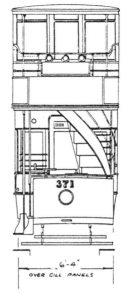

371

6'-4"
OVER CILL PANELS

Plan of D1 class tramcar

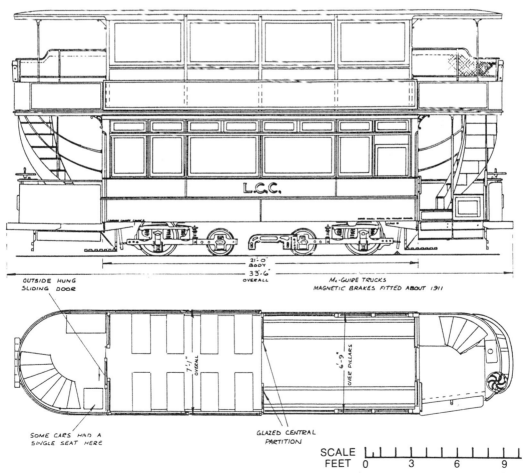

L.C.C.

21'-0" BODY
33'-6" OVERALL

OUTSIDE HUNG SLIDING DOOR

McGUIRE TRUCKS
MAGNETIC BRAKES FITTED ABOUT 1911

7'-1" OVERALL

6'-9" OVER PILLARS

SOME CARS HAD A SINGLE SEAT HERE

GLAZED CENTRAL PARTITION

SCALE
FEET 0   3   6   9

Car 2

This tram was delivered from Charlton Works in February 1935. It received the trucks and some electrical equipment from damaged car 1370, but the bodywork was substantially new incorporating an Alpax aluminium alloy top deck with domed roof. The lower saloon featured swivelling seats supplied by the G.D.Peters Company. The reconditioning programme adopted by London Transport eventually dealt with around 150 tramcars; more information on these "rehab" cars can be found in companion album *Lewisham and Catford Tramways*. Car 2 ended its days at Abbey Wood Depot after spells at New Cross and Norwood. Its fate was not as kind as its more famous sister car 1 (which was preserved), and it was destroyed by fire at Penhall Road scrap yard.

Plan of London Transport car 2.

scale feet

London Transport

E/1 car 2

... but Hovis and butter is better

LONDON TRANSPORT

Upper Deck

Lower Deck

115. Alone of the reconditioned trams in the fleet, car 2 managed to survive right to the end of tramway operation in the capital on 5th July 1952.   (R.B.Parr)

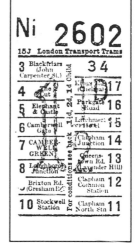

116. Note that the panel below the right hand driver's windscreen of car 2 has been repaired after accident damage; a strip of creased rexine material has been fixed between the top of the dash and the windscreen. Unfortunately this proceedure was only too typical of the "make do and mend" philosophy practised by LT in respect of its tramways.   (J.C.Gillham)

117. The top deck of car 2 has echoes of LCC prototype car 1 with the domed ceiling and lights affixed to sloping panels above the windows. (J.C.Gillham)

118. The two and one configuration of lower saloon seats allowed more space for standing passengers at peak times. Only a handful of London trams were equipped with swivelling seats as opposed to the more conventional variety where the backs were flipped over by the conductor so that passengers could face the direction of travel. The arrangement depicted here, where a foot pedal was depressed to turn the seat, was unpopular with conductors as it added to the turn round time at each terminus. The seats also had to be manoeuvred in a fixed sequence. On services 36, 38, 44 and 46 this was only half a problem as reversals on these services occurred normally at Abbey Wood, Middle Park Avenue and Southwark Bridge respectively, the other terminus being a loop at either the Embankment or Beresford Square. (J.C.Gillham)

ABBEY WOOD, CAMBERWELL, CLAPHAM, HAMMERSMITH, HANWELL, NEW CROSS, NORWOOD, PURLEY, STREATHAM, THORNTON HEATH AND WANDSWORTH.

CONVERSION TO TROLLEYBUS—WANDSWORTH AREA.

On Sunday, 12th September, 1937, the following alterations to routes will take place.

TRAM ROUTES CURTAILED.

Route No.	Curtailed to operate between :—
12	Hop Exchange and Wandsworth High Street.
14	Hop Exchange and Battersea, " Princes Head."
26	Hop Exchange and Clapham Junction.
28	Victoria and Clapham Junction.
6	City (via Southwark) and Tooting, Amen Corner.
31	Hackney (Clarence Road) and Battersea, " Princes Head."

Tram Route 30 will be withdrawn.

TROLLEYBUS ROUTES TO COMMENCE OPERATION.

Route No.	Route.
612	Battersea, " Princes Head," and Fair Green, Mitcham.
626	Clapham Junction and Acton Market Place, via Harlesden (peak hours only).
628	Clapham Junction and Craven Park Junction.
630	Harrow Road (Scrubs Lane) and West Croydon Station.

FINALE

119. The motorman of this tram crossing Putney Bridge casts a glance at the replacement trolleybus on a test run in September 1937. In a few days the end will come and the disused tramtracks will acquire a veneer of rust before they are covered with tarmac. Some miles of metal still lie dormant under London's streets, but the rails abandoned in the post-war conversion were mostly lifted with the road surface being reinstated afterwards. (K.H.Rudolph)

120. The shadows lengthen as car 1752 passes on one of the last runs before this section of service 28 is converted to trolleybuses. (A.B.Cross)

SOUTH LONDON TRAMWAYS CO.

Qa

FARE 1d

TO OR FROM

Wandsworth
and
'Prince's Head' Tavern

Plough Lane
and
Brighton Railway Stn.

'Prince's Head' Tavern
and
Nine Elms Lane.

This Ticket is available for a SINGLE journey only — on the Car where issued. It must be produced for inspection on demand of the Conductor or other Official of the Company. Any passenger attempting to use this Ticket for a SECOND journey, or otherwise defrauding the Company, will be liable to Prosecution, and a fine of FORTY SHILLINGS. (See Bye-laws.)